Test Your Baby

RACHEL FEDERMAN
ILLUSTRATIONS BY
ELLEN T. CRENSHAW

HARPER

For Ellie & Leah, my original guinea pigs

HarperCollins*Publishers*
1 London Bridge Street
London SE1 9GF
www.harpercollins.co.uk

First published by HarperCollins*Publishers*
in 2016

1 3 5 7 9 10 8 6 4 2

Text copyright © 2016 Rachel Federman
Illustrations by Ellen T. Crenshaw
Interior design: Rosamund Saunders
Cover images © Shutterstock

A catalogue record for this book is
available from the British Library

ISBN 978-0-00-820022-0

Printed and bound in the UK

DISCLAIMER: This is a book of
humour. Caution should be used in all
activities, and safety and responsibility
rest with the reader. The author and
publisher do not accept responsibility
for injury or damage.

MIX
Paper from
responsible sources
FSC™ C007454

FSC™ is a non-profit international organisation established to promote the responsible
management of the world's forests. Products carrying the FSC label are independently certified
to assure consumers that they come from forests that are managed to meet the social, economic
and ecological needs of present and future generations.

Contents

Introduction

It's never too early to start testing your baby. In fact hopefully you're reading this book in the delivery room, because it can be too late. Gone are the carefree days when all you had to worry about as a new parent was how to feed an inconsolable baby, survive on no sleep, install a car seat, assemble a high chair, change nappies round the clock and treat a potentially infected umbilical cord. No longer can you loll away the blissful early days rocking your howling, colicky infant into the briefest of naps, passively wait for him to reach outdated milestones like holding up his neck and learning to crawl. Playtime is not for playing any more. He needs to hold his own in a debate about foreign policy, not just hold up his neck. He has to learn the back crawl in Baby Swim class, not just the forward crawl on land.

And forget bedtime stories about anthropomorphised bears getting into their pyjamas. Those kinds of stories simply don't provide enough intellectual stimulation for today's child, who should at a minimum be able to identify all eight bear species by paw print and be conversant with the changing hibernation patterns of all before his second birthday. Where once at mealtimes you might have simply narrated in a sing-songy voice, 'The spoon goes in the mouth', you now need to specify the velocity of the spoon, provide Latin names for body parts and set puréed vegetables in their proper historical context.

And I hope you've already introduced the baby to a range of musical composers and literary genres in utero. Upon arrival, a full-term baby should be comfortable distinguishing between late Baroque and early Renaissance periods of Western music, for example, and between the Enlightenment and Victorian eras of literature, taking into account certain persistent strains of Romantic thought.

Wait. I know what you're thinking. You don't have a spare minute to take a shower let alone conduct elaborate psychometrically sound tests. These tests are simple and quick to perform. You can conduct one, two or a whole chapter at a time – whatever you and your baby have the time and energy for. Just make a note of the results and return to the book when you are ready.

In the following pages, I'll take you through the major areas of your baby's day, beginning with a general overview and moving on to Playtime, Mealtimes and Sleeping. I also want to know how your pride and joy performs in the outside world, so I've included all-important questions about library storytime and visiting the playground under the section called

Outings. And because I feel that a deep appreciation for arts and literature is fundamental to the proper cultivation of any human whose life is still measured in months or even weeks, I've included a chapter on this topic as well. While the questions in these sections ask you to speculate about your

baby's behaviour and responses based on your observations thus far, the final chapter, Activity Exam, requires you to actually set up a trial and observe your baby.

I hope you have fun along the way. We're not really assessing your baby's skills so much as hoping to offer some insight into what areas might particularly engage her. Is she a genius? Of course! Every child is born a genius. And there's really nothing you need to do to improve that potential but take care of your precious bundle of never-ending needs and give it lots of love, even as you complain daily about the incredible demands of parenting. Most important for the purpose of these tests, please supervise your little one at all times. Only you know what your baby is and is not capable of; please don't put him in any situation that is not developmentally appropriate, and please don't take silly ideas as serious suggestions (no hot and spicy aloo tikki for your six-month-old, for example).

Try to resist the pressure to race your baby through babyhood, and toddler through toddlerhood, and child through childhood. If you can slow down enough to meaningfully engage with your baby, which I hope this book helps you to do, then you're ready to run your own victory lap.

Chapter One

Everyday with Your Baby

The bright side of the endless fatigue of the early months of parenting is that when you're up at 5am every day you really make the most of the mornings. And the mid-mornings. And the late mornings. And the early afternoons. And the fact that an hour seems to go by ... so ... incredibly ... slowly. Enjoy these Zen moments. Babies keep you tethered to the present – there's really no other choice! There's no time for daydreaming while staring out of the window or dwelling on the past. You're lucky if you can find a moment to snap a picture for a baby book. Let's find out what life is like with your whiz-kid in training right now. It's hard to imagine, but as plodding as it now feels, it will all go by in a blur.

1. When it comes to your daily schedule, does your baby prefer:

A Sticking to a routine? ☐

B Unexpected visits and spontaneous trips? ☐

C A mix of structure and spontaneity? ☐

D Reading lots of books on time management and taking the best practices from each? ☐

E Sleep. Eat. Play. Repeat? ☐

2. Which part of your baby book was hardest to fill out?

A The first time he sat up (he never sits still for long enough) ☐

B The first day home from hospital (I was asleep) ☐

C A hand print (he didn't like the feel of the non-toxic stamp pad) ☐

D The first smile (haven't seen one yet) ☐

E Favourite games (he's chess-obsessed and I'm still figuring out how the pieces move) ☐

3. In which position does your baby most like to be held?

A The rugby ball ☐

B The cradle ☐

C The two-arm upright chest hug ☐

D The over-the-shoulder snuggle ☐

E Out facing the world ☐

A

B

C

D

E

15

4. How does your baby indicate she no longer wants to be held?

A Whine ☐

B Whimper ☐

C Scream ☐

D Groin kick (or, in official Baby Karate lingo, 'Kin Geri') ☐

E Polite request for change of scenery ☐

5. Using the Volcanic Explosivity Index developed in 1982 (adapted for your child), when do eruptions tend to be greatest?

A Mealtimes ☐

B Naptimes ☐

C Company overstaying their welcome ☐

D Wanted the blue spoon not the green spoon ☐

E No discernible pattern ☐

6. Which law does your baby best dramatise?

A The law of inertia ☐

B The law of gravity ☐

C The law against trespassing ☐

D Murphy's Law ☐

E The law of super-long naps on days you are in a rush to get somewhere ☐

7. Which task is hardest to accomplish when taking care of your baby?

A Changing her nappy ☐

B Feeding her ☐

C Getting her dressed ☐

D Getting her undressed ☐

E Not going crazy because you feel as though you are getting absolutely nothing done ☐

8. What did you not expect when you knew you were expecting?

A How much advice strangers would feel the need to give you □

B The pleasant buzzing sensation of intense sleep deprivation □

C How much of a workout you would get from bouncing the bouncy seat with your foot □

D How good puréed banana would taste □

E How many different types of unidentified stains can originate from one 4-kg (9-lb) creature □

9. When she was young enough to make involuntary movements with her arms, what did she most resemble?

A An orchestra conductor ☐

B A butterfly ☐

C Your year-two science teacher ☐

D A pterodactyl ☐

E Michelle Pfeiffer as Titania, Queen of the Fairies, in Michael Hoffman's 1999 version of 'A Midsummer Night's Dream' ☐

10. Which object in your handbag is he most desperate to get his hands on?

A Keys ☐

B Phone ☐

C Pen ☐

D Cheque book ☐

E Scuba gear ☐

Chapter Two

PLAYTIME

Remember when I explained that playtime is not just for playing any more? Now it's the time for strengthening gross motor skills and practising fine motor skills, not to mention enhancing coordination, flexibility and sensory engagement. Well, really, it's always been about those things – we just didn't know as much about them before. So what is your baby noticing and taking in? Let's find out what kinds of things make her want to jump in the game.

1. What is your baby's favourite use for a ball?

A Rolling it ☐

B Listening to a story about it ☐

C Trying to balance it on her head ☐

D Trading it for another toy in the playground ☐

E Chasing it ☐

2. Which toy instrument is his favourite?

A Xylophone ☐

B Cowbell ☐

C Drums ☐

D Piano ☐

E His uncle's 1962 Fender Strat ☐

3. When your baby first learned to crawl, what non-human creature did she most resemble?

A Worm ☐

B Crab ☐

C Woodlouse, AKA roly poly ☐

D Slug ☐

E Panther ☐

4. If he were in a Disney movie, which character would he be?

A Goofy ☐

B Buzz Lightyear ☐

C Tinkerbell ☐

D Simba ☐

E Merida from *Brave* ☐

5. When you sing nursery rhymes together, which hand motions come most naturally?

A Rowing your boat ☐

B Hokey Cokey ☐

C Spinning hands for 'Wheels on the Bus' ☐

D Thumbs up for 'Where is Thumbkin?' ☐

E He prefers full-body 'Gangnam Style' to nursery rhymes ☐

6. When you play peek-a-boo together, does your baby:

A Giggle? ☐

B Cry? ☐

C Imitate you? ☐

D Imitate you but peek before it's time to say boo? ☐

E Run off? ☐

7. Which of the following would most engage your baby's attention?

A You singing 'I'm a Little Teapot' ☐

B A traditional Japanese tea ceremony ☐

C Someone making a rocket balloon ☐

D Ted Talks on productivity ☐

E A high-stakes poker game ☐

8. Which song or type of music makes her want to dance?

A Mozart's 'Rondo Alla Turca' ☐

B 'Uptown Funk' by Mark Ronson featuring Bruno Mars ☐

C Bette Midler's 'Hello in There' ☐

D Anything from Nirvana's *In Utero* album ☐

E She prefers silence and bare feet – kind of a modern performance piece aesthetic ☐

9. Does your baby seem to like a break from sensory input?

A Not very often, but after a long stretch of new sights and activities he needs a siesta ☐

B He can only tolerate short stretches of activity before he needs to meditate ☐

C He'd be at home in Times Square or Piccadilly Circus ☐

D He likes to alternate between stimulation and quiet ☐

E He prefers solitude and quiet for baby reflection ☐

10. Does your baby seem aware of other babies?

A Only the one in the mirror ☐

B She's better at small talk than I am ☐

C The quiet ones intrigue her ☐

D She's a bit shy at first but warms up during
tummy time ☐

E She finds them a bit dull and prefers to hang with the
3+ group ☐

Chapter Three

ARTS AND LITERATURE

Broad exposure to arts and literature in the early years will boost your baby's language skills and vocabulary, reading comprehension, critical thinking and multicultural awareness. Plus, a casual mention in the playground of a recent poem from *The London Review of Books* or current exhibit at the Tate will quickly establish him as a member of the infant intelligentsia.

1. Which show do you think will best hold your child's attention when she's a bit older?

A Anything with music ☐

B Anything with aliens ☐

C Anything on the history channel ☐

D Reruns of *The Office* ☐

E Videos from the delivery room on the day she was born ☐

2. If there were baby versions of these reality shows, on which one would your baby star?

A Robot Wars ☐

B The Bachelor ☐

C Britain's Got Talent ☐

D MasterChef ☐

E The Island with Bear Grylls ☐

3. Which of the following best describes your baby's foreign language facility?

A He has a working knowledge of French ☐

B He can recognise the word for 'milk' in at least five languages ☐

C He can say 'Pick me up' in sign language ☐

D He is familiar with several obsolete languages ☐

E I'm more focused on trying to learn his ☐

4. How would your baby translate 'moo shoo ga ga'?

A The Second Law of Thermodynamics ☐

B Is the universe infinite? ☐

C Sorry you hate your boss ☐

D Do we have a deal? ☐

E Can we order Chinese food tonight? ☐

5. At which section of the art gallery is your baby most likely to perk up?

A Postmodernism, but before a heavy emphasis on the pastiche ☐

B Art of the Early Roman Empire ☐

C Surrealists ('Dada' in particular, of course) ☐

D The Rooftop Bar (good networking op) ☐

E Sculpture and Decorative Art (so many breakable things!) ☐

6. Does your child prefer to read:

A Counting books? ☐

B Books about existentialism? ☐

C Cookbooks? ☐

D The *Times*? ☐

E Anything written on a papyrus scroll? ☐

7. If your baby saw a painting by Jackson Pollock, what would she say if she could speak?

A Let's calculate the kinetic energy ☐

B He could use some more blue ☐

C How come he's allowed to drip everywhere? ☐

D The movie didn't do him justice ☐

E How much is it worth? ☐

8. What intrigues your baby most about playing with an alphabet puzzle?

A Trying to learn the names of the letters ☐

B Trying to get the pieces in the right place ☐

C Making her own sculpture ☐

D Researching the history of the wooden puzzle ☐

E Hiding the pieces all around the living room ☐

9. What costume would your baby like best for Halloween?

A The flapper costume you wore as a child ☐

B A shop-bought Superman ☐

C A homemade, Pinterest-worthy bumblebee outfit ☐

D Something esoteric like Shakespeare that other babies won't recognise ☐

E Going as himself ☐

10. If you gave your child a bucket of water, a paintbrush and a sheet of paper, would she:

A Tip over the water and try to sell you a new brand of paper towels? ☐

B Attempt to plunge your phone in the water? ☐

C Recreate the Pollock you showed her in Question 7? ☐

D Ask if you have a psychrometer to measure humidity? ☐

E Ask whether the bucket is half empty or half full? ☐

Chapter Four

MEALTIMES

At first babies feed pretty much on demand. Some master-caretakers are able to get them on to a schedule fairly quickly, with three-hour intervals between feedings, but for most it's at some point in the fourth month that something like a schedule begins to emerge, when certain larger feedings could possibly be called mealtimes. Table manners can't reasonably be expected for another few years, but the plus side is that babies aren't too picky (if you've never had anything but milk, then puréed carrots and kale are going to taste pretty damn good!). Let's find out about your baby's likes and dislikes at this oh-so-important time of the day, if only because it means you might actually get a chance to sit down.

1. How quickly did your baby learn to breast- or bottle-feed?

A Just after the placenta arrived ☐

B When she started to grasp the concept of infinity ☐

C We're still working with a consultant ☐

D She runs an online breast-feeding class for newborns ☐

E You honestly expect me to remember anything that happened in those first few weeks? ☐

2. What is your baby's favourite food? (Speak with your doctor about when to introduce new foods; please make your best guess for this question.)

A Rice cereal ☐

B Sweet potato purée from a jar ☐

C Organic peach spinach quinoa squeeze ☐

D Homemade mango avocado purée ☐

E Spicy aloo tikki from Curry-in-a-Hurry ☐

3. Does your baby show interest when you're preparing something to eat?

A There's nothing she likes better than the pop of a baby food jar opening ☐

B Only if it's a recipe I haven't tried before, preferably something from scratch ☐

C She pretends not to be interested, but I feel her critical gaze when my julienned veggies aren't uniform ☐

D Her main interest is needing something from me at the most crucial moment of any recipe ☐

E Not really, she's too fascinated by the ceiling ☐

4. In between meals, what does your baby most like to suck on?

A Dummy ☐

B Finger ☐

C Blanket ☐

D Spoon ☐

E Bottle ☐

5. Pick the image that best represents the area around your baby's high chair after a meal.

Chapter Five

OUTINGS

The only thing harder than staying inside with a baby all day is trying to get outside with said howling baby. You will inevitably forget either the nappies or the wipes or the non-toxic suncream or the non-toxic insect repellent (if he is even old enough to wear either one) or the bottle or the sippy cup or the sling or the thing you wear over your shoulder so you can breast-feed discreetly. Sometimes you'll go back and get the thing you forgot, but more often than not you'll stretch the meaning of 'make do' beyond anything it was ever intended to mean. What kind of outings does your baby like? How does she interact with strangers? What would he order in a café if he could? Let's find out.

1. Let loose in an indoor playroom, your baby makes a beeline for:

A A pretend cash register? ☐

B A dollshouse? ☐

C An Etch-a-Sketch? ☐

D The loudest or most dangerous thing in the room? ☐

E The exit sign? ☐

2. When you go outside and point to a tree, does your baby:

A Look at the tree? ☐

B Look at your hand? ☐

C Look at his own hand? ☐

D Fall asleep? ☐

E Burp? ☐

3. Where are you most likely to find your little one on a Saturday evening? ☐

A At a Baby Disco ☐

B Chilling at home watching something on CBeebies ☐

C Getting a foot massage ☐

D Just waking up from an awkwardly late nap, which means you'll have absolutely no time to yourself all evening ☐

E Whining, trying to put stuff she shouldn't in her mouth, wanting food but then not eating anything, wanting a bottle but not drinking anything, managing to spill stuff out of a no-spill cup ... ☐

4. At which baby class do you think your baby would show the most promise?

A Messy Art ☐

B Tadpole Swim ☐

C Baby Gymnastics (watching the baby roll around on the floor just like she would at home, but paying extra money for the additional obstacles of other infants rolling around) ☐

D Storytime ☐

E Beginner Metaphysics ☐

5. How does your baby like to play on a swing?

A Gentle and slow ☐

B He's fine to sit still and enjoy the view ☐

C He'd prefer to help me push the swing, pretending there's a baby in there ☐

D I can't get him away from the kids with the trading cards long enough to swing ☐

E High and fast like the big kids ☐

6. At library storytime, which part does your baby like best?

A When you play 'Pat a Cake' ☐

B When the librarian explains that the original copyright title of the popular 'ABC' song was 'The ABC, a German air with variations for the flute with an easy accompaniment for the piano forte' ☐

C When she gets a sticker at the end ☐

D When the librarian blows bubbles ☐

E When she gets to play horsey on your lap ☐

7. Does your baby feel comfortable around strangers?

A She's friendly, but keeps her distance ☐

B She's comfortable, but quick to find fault ☐

C She engages in lengthy debates about the merits of breast- over bottle-feeding ☐

D If by comfortable you mean emits blood-curdling screams the minute they enter the room, then yes ☐

E She's fidgety, but only because she hates small talk with people she doesn't know ☐

8. Which book would friends recommend to you after observing your interactions with your baby?

A *The Happiest Baby on the Block* ☐

B *The Guy's Guide to Surviving Pregnancy and the First Year of Childhood* ☐

C *Daddy Needs a Drink* ☐

D *The Guide to Baby Sleep Positions: Survival Tips for Co-Sleeping Parents* ☐

E *The Hot Mama's Handbook* ☐

9. Does your little one like to play pass-the-baby with random people when you take him to a party?

A He's usually up for a brief round, but only until the appetisers are served ☐

B As long as we keep up a 4/4 rhythm ☐

C He kicks most guests in the face ☐

D He forgets me by the third person who grabs hold of him ☐

E He doesn't enjoy it, but tolerates it with a stoic expression ☐

10. If your baby could order for herself in a café, what would she order?

A Apple juice ☐

B Chocolate chip cookie ☐

C Mashed banana ☐

D Café au lait – hold the café? ☐

E Triple espresso with an extra shot ☐

Chapter Six

SLEEPING

I know, I know, it doesn't feel like it – but believe it or not, your infant will actually sleep for much of the day. People will tell you to 'sleep when the baby sleeps', but what they don't take into account is that if you sleep when the baby sleeps, you'll literally have no time for self-indulgent things like taking a shower or paying your bills. In the beginning, let them sleep. But how does your baby like to fall asleep? And what is it like reading books before bed? Here are five questions about your baby's favourite bedtime pastimes.

1. What's the best way to get your baby to fall asleep?

A A walk in the pram ☐

B Swaddle him up and he'll sleep anywhere, kind of like my ex-boyfriend ☐

C Lullabies in a quiet room ☐

D Jukebox blasting in a crowded bar ☐

E No idea, but when you find out, let me know ☐

2. Does your baby show a preference for what she wears to sleep?

A Nah, she's happy in hand-me-down pjs, or even just a nappy ☐

B I have to put her in at least a onesie, otherwise she'll take her nappy off ☐

C She likes something outrageously cute with animal ears (and insists on parading around for everyone to oooh and ahh) ☐

D She can't get a wink without her Bill Gates bodysuit ☐

E Prefers T-shirts with inappropriate sayings about parents who drink too much ☐

3. Does your baby sleep for long stretches at a time?

A He'll give me a nice two-hour stretch if the phone doesn't wake him up ☐

B He prefers to cat nap ☐

C He prefers to dog nap ☐

D If the doctor hadn't told us to wake him every three hours, he'd practically hibernate ☐

E If he stays in motion, he'll sink into a deep sleep. In his cot, he pops up like a jack-in-the-box ☐

4. When you read a story before bed, which would your baby rather you do?

A Read a familiar book and stick exactly to the text ☐

B Read a familiar book but improvise a bit, adding the wrong words here and there ☐

C Read a new children's book from the library ☐

D Read part of what you are currently reading (not super high-brow literary, but still, something respectable) ☐

E Read part of what you are currently reading (when you're willing to admit that you only ever read gossip mags and comic books) ☐

5. In *Goodnight Moon*, which part does your baby like best?

A The red balloon ☐

B The rotary phone ☐

C The bowl full of mush ☐

D Searching for the mouse in every picture ☐

E Figuring out where in the northern hemisphere the great green room is located based on the constellations and the position of the moon ☐

Activity Exam

These questions require you to set up a trial and participate in the activities with your baby. Only you can decide what is safe and developmentally appropriate for your child; it goes without saying that you should only engage in activities that fall within this realm. Do not try anything that sounds questionable. Before you begin, take a look at your weekly schedule to determine the hours available for optimal assessment.

Tips for Getting the Best Results

1. Find a time when you and your baby have both had a good night's rest.

2. Make sure your baby is clean and dry, not plagued by either a nappy rash or a head cold.

3. Find a day that's not too hot. Babies can easily grow uncomfortable in excessive heat and may be unusually fussy.

4. Find a place that's quiet, protected from disturbing noises such as that of a crying baby.

5. Ideally, conduct the tests after the umbilical cord has fallen off but before teething begins.

6. Make sure your baby is well fed.

7. Begin the tests only when you have had enough time to recover from the birth, but before all the help from friends and relatives has fully dropped off.

8. Perform the tests on a day when you have no other pressing tasks on the agenda.

1. Roll a soft ball to your baby. Does he:

A Roll it back to you? ☐

B Sit on it? ☐

C Throw it back to you? ☐

D Take it and score a try? ☐

E Move to a hardwood floor to reduce friction? ☐

2. Show your baby her reflection in a mirror. Which face most resembles her expression?

A Baby looks angry, shaking fist in a 'You lookin' at me?' expression ☐

B Huge smile ☐

C Confusion ☐

D Surprise ☐

E Maybe an emoticon holding a sign that says 'Help' ☐

3. Hold your index finger out for your little one. Does he:

A Grab on? ☐

B Hold his index finger out? ☐

C Play 'Where is Thumbkin?' ☐

D Say 'I'll take one'? ☐

E Ask what you're pointing at? ☐

4. Get out your stopwatch and observe your baby for a full three minutes. Which activity does he spend the most time doing?

A Babbling ☐

B Blinking ☐

C Stretching his fingers ☐

D Kicking his legs ☐

E Trying to grab the stopwatch ☐

5. Read the following quotes out loud and try to gauge your baby's reaction. Depending on her age, you may notice enhanced eye contact, excited movements, a focused expression, a smile or even clapping. Which quote does your baby find most inspiring? Make sure to pause for a moment between quotes.

A There are only two ways to live your life. One is as though nothing is a miracle. The other is as though everything is a miracle. – *Albert Einstein* ☐

B If you know the point of balance you can settle the details. If you can settle the details, you can stop running around. Your mind will become calm. If your mind becomes calm, you can think in front of a tiger. If you can think in front of a tiger, you will surely succeed. – *Mencius* ☐

C The universe is made of stories, not of atoms.
– *Muriel Rukeyser* ☐

D The obscure we see eventually. The completely obvious, it seems, takes longer. – *Edward R. Murrow* ☐

E Two roads diverged in a wood, and I – I took the one less travelled by, and that has made all the difference.
– *Robert Frost* ☐

6. This question attempts to measure your baby's response to learning about object permanence. Show him a toy and let him feel it and hold it. Then take the toy and hide it under a blanket. After 30 seconds or so, take the toy back out. What is his reaction?

A A detached kind of ennui and vague reference to John Locke ☐

B Mild amusement ☐

C Surprise or confusion ☐

D Tell you he's got more toys like it in the back ☐

E He's still crying because I took the toy away ☐

7. Ask your baby to roll over. Does she:

A Roll halfway and roll back again? ☐

B Roll all the way round? ☐

C Break into a lively version of 'Like a Rolling Stone'? ☐

D Explain the benefits of rolling over your minutes on your network plan from one month to the next? ☐

E Perform a flawless floor routine, complete with back handspring? ☐

8. Use a puppet to talk to your baby. Have the puppet say 'hello' and ask your baby how he is. How does your baby react?

A He giggles ☐

B He swats the puppet away ☐

C He attempts to shake the puppet's hand and/or says 'hello' back ☐

D He tells you to work on your ventriloquism skills ☐

E He raises concerns about the possibility that you are a puppet ruler and he is pulling all the strings ☐

Analysing Your Baby's Score

Mostly As – Scientist/Scholar

Your baby's favourite place is surrounded by board books, and most of the time he doesn't even chew them. For all his actions, he knows there's an equal and opposite reaction, and he's just as eager to take things apart to see how they work as he is to put things together. When you go star-gazing, he'll be more interested in how fast light travels than the names of the constellations. And he'll find the mechanics of the digestive system more interesting than what he's having for dinner. While other babies collect stuffed animals, he'll collect data for his latest research, and the fact that he loves to see things implode, explode, break down, rearrange and transform can make for an exhausting day. Just make sure he gets enough time studying cloud formations for fun and not for a publishable study on climate change. As much as he craves new knowledge, he'll enjoy a walk in the park or a play on the swings as much as any other baby. And you always knew you'd learn at least as much from him as the other way around. Just as atoms bond, so will the two of you, knowing every day is an experiment, with an outcome we can only imagine.

Mostly Bs – Philosopher

Your baby might knock over her sippy cup like any other member of the under-one set, but not without musing on the meaning of emptiness. She faces her days with a calm equanimity, able to step back from lost tempers or lost bottles to consider big-life questions that are often submerged under the day-to-day demands of life as a tiny person just learning to use a spoon. She's more interested in the size of the universe than the size of her rice cereal and can amuse herself almost anywhere, staring at a mobile or a mirror, as she contemplates the meaning of the phrase 'I blink, therefore I am'.

Mostly Cs – Creator/Entertainer

Her ultrasound image was her first moment in the limelight, and she hasn't stopped performing since. She's the baby babbling the loudest, flailing the most flamboyantly, wearing the brightest costume and keeping all your guests amused, even when you're not. She changes naptimes and perks up her ears when you try a new recipe for mashed pears and sweet potatoes. She signals her likes and dislikes with confidence, adapts to new situations, is open to experiment and loves it when you introduce her to any art, music or other cultural experience. Sure, Jazz for Newborns might seem like an oxymoron (after all, you're still getting the hang of syncopation yourself), but there's a lot she can get out of it, starting with trying to convince you she 'Ain't Misbehavin'' (you already know 'It's a Wonderful World' with her). Sometimes you hear applause when all you want to hear is a gentle round of 'Pat a Cake', but remember, you always have the best seat in the house.

Mostly Ds – Entrepreneur

Business opportunities abound for your industrial baby, who is more interested in making a trade than a snake out of Play-Doh. Don't be surprised if he's the baby handing out toys in the playroom or telling tots whose turn it is to go down the slide. He's got a high tolerance for risk, excellent social skills and an uncanny ability to scope out potential investors in his Hot Cross Buns (but watch out, he's likely to raise the price from one-a-penny and don't expect any two-a-penny deals). He'll keep you on schedule, and will most likely be up for trying all the latest baby toys and gear, but he'll be more interested in filling a niche than in actually wearing a knitted hat.

Mostly Es – Explorer

Like all babies, yours is desperate to find out more about the world, although in her case, the adventure never ends. While other babies roll around the infant play area, content with the soft toys and gentle rattles, yours is the one making a beeline for the big-kid train table, always curious about what lies beyond. She'll love new sights, new smells, new textures and sounds, and the flip side of her need for stimulation is that you won't be limited by her need for any kind of downtime. Just pack enough water and snacks, a change of clothes, a swimsuit (always carry one), and plan to stay out all day as you pursue her quest to leave no Lego unturned.

Conclusion

Before you have a baby yourself, you see one in a pram or bouncy chair and think that taking care of one doesn't look particularly hard. Sure, the new parents you know look like they've been through hell, but those are low-energy people. If and when you ever have a baby, you'll be fine. You've pulled all-nighters before and you've got a high tolerance for incredibly annoying high-pitched sounds ...

Then you have a baby. And just getting through the day is the hardest thing you've ever done. I really believe that one of the things that makes it so incredibly difficult at present is that the stakes have changed and that many caretakers are isolated. You don't have parents and uncles and cousins around to help with the kids, or even to get dinner started while you fuss with the kids or throw in a load of washing.

Another important factor is the expectation that you will be cultivating your offspring from conception into a high-achieving prodigy. In my first year back at work after my son was born, a colleague gave me an educational baby DVD. I hadn't even heard of those, but who doesn't like the idea of a baby effortlessly learning to speak Chinese in the evening while you drink wine and chop up onions for dinner? Except the DVD was aimed at zero-to-three-month-olds. I panicked. My son was almost ten months old by that point. I had already missed a crucial early-learning window! What was my son supposed to have learned that all the other babies had already mastered? What colours and shapes was he missing out on? Is there any way he could possibly catch up?

As I raced the one-mile walk home, I imagined every baby I passed to be fluent in not only Chinese, but sign language and Spanish, able to recognise exotic animal sounds, sing opera and count to 1,000 with ease, while all my little guy could do was run around the apartment and put things in his mouth. These brainy Einstein babies would laugh at mine, lap him in Baby Physics, out-perform him in playgroup ... Why hadn't anyone told me about these DVDs earlier?

My son was happy when I got into the apartment, clapping along as my husband played the guitar. I caught my breath and kept the DVD hidden away. That night I read the research that says babies who watch these kinds of educational videos gain no advantage and in fact know on average significantly fewer words than babies who don't watch them. Watching DVDs, it turns out, was not only unhelpful, but maybe even harmful. What about being in the room while other people were watching a DVD or TV? What about certain types of music? The general cacophony of living in New York? What effect might that have on stress levels for infants? Maybe we should be out in the country, away from all the stimuli of the city and the ambitious hyper-parents. (In short, I swung totally the other way, instantaneously.)

So began a dynamic that continues to this day – wondering what other parents are doing for their children that I'm not, then finding out that those celebrated trendy approaches may not be ideal. Sometimes I find myself feeling critical of 'helicopter' mums – those who want to control everything. But then, I realise, I might just be a different version. Even if my idea of control is letting a baby fall and get up by himself, I'm still overthinking lots of stuff, trying to create the exact right environment.

A friend told me recently that maybe we shouldn't worry about creating the exact right environment. Maybe we should aim for stability and time. That baby of mine who missed out on the genius-inducing potential of the educational DVDs is now in primary school, happily dashing into the playground after school with a younger sister already out of babyhood as well. And I've been lucky to get to spend so much time having fun with them.

I hope you are able to spend time having fun with your babies, too. I hope you take the questions and activities suggested in this book as an opening towards true engagement, rather than an invitation to enhance their CVs or jump-start their university applications. Expanding their reach, not reaching milestones, should be the goal. In the age of high-stakes testing that often stifles true learning, these assessments are meant to be fun and to give you a chance to learn about your baby's interests and natural abilities. All babies and children are naturally eager to learn. All we have to do is make sure they're healthy and safe, and get out of their way.

Afterward:

You and Your Baby

For fun, find out if your six-month-old might one day create an artistic masterpiece or prove we are living in a multiverse. While you're at it, I hope you are able to slow down long enough, and turn your attention away from the wired world fully enough, to enjoy these fleeting days. The research clearly shows that caretaker engagement with babies and toddlers is highly correlated with achievement further down the line. By making time for sustained engagement with your little ones, you'll give them the best chance for reaching their full potential as adults. Plus, you'll get to witness and learn from one of the greatest achievements by far of early childhood – the ability to live purely in the moment.

Bibliography

Acredolo, Linda and Goodwyn, Susan, both PhD, *Baby Minds: Brain-Building Games Your Baby Will Love*, Random House, 2000

Chang, Kenneth, 'Gauging the Intelligence of Infants,' *New York Times*, 7 April 2014

Kennedy, Michelle, *The Big Book of Happy: 500 Games & Activities for Ages 2 to 6*, Ivy Press, 2008

Gardner, Howard E, *Multiple Intelligences: New Horizons in Theory and Practice*, Basic Books, 2006

Nurk, Dr. Cindy Bunin, *Fun with Mommy & Me*, Dutton, 1993

Sternberg, Robert J, *Beyond IQ: A Triarchic Theory of Human Intelligence*, Cambridge University Press, 1984

Warner, Penny, *Baby Play & Learn*, MJF Books, 1999

ACKNOWLEDGEMENTS

Thanks to Caitlin – editor extraordinaire – for her creative ideas, last-minute saves and incredible patience, and to Ellen for bringing the text to life with her illustrations. Thanks also to the rest of the editorial, design and production team who quietly put in the hard work of book-making mostly behind the scenes.